# Stories

Pen  hill

Please return / renew this item by last
date shown. Books may also be renewed
by phone or the Internet.

Northamptonshire Libraries and Information Service

Northamptonshire
County Council

www.northamptonshire.gov.uk/catalogue

A & C Black · London

Designed by Jane Warring

Illustrations by Lindy Norton

Children's pictures by
Amber Civardi, Charlotte Downham, Lara Haworth, Lucinda Howell,
Sophie Johns, Julia Luther, Lucy MacDonald Watson,
India Masson-Taylor, Zoe More O'Ferrall, Gussie Pownhall,
Thomas Stofer, Alice Williams, Jessica Williams

Picture research by Sara Elliott

Photographs by Peter Millard

Reprinted 1999, 2002
First paperback edition 1996
First published 1996 in hardback by
A & C Black Publishers Ltd
37 Soho Square, London, W1D 3QZ
www.acblack.com

Created by
Thumbprint Books

Copyright © 1996 Thumbprint Books

A CIP catalogue record for this book is available from the British Library

ISBN 0-7136-6699-4

Printed and bound in Singapore

A & C Black uses paper produced with elemental chlorine-free pulp,
harvested from managed, sustainable forests.

*Cover photograph:* The Harvest, 1989, is a Peruvian Arpillera (appliqué).
Women throughout Latin America make embroidery pictures, like this, to tell
stories about their life in villages and on farms. Women's organisations sell them to
help raise money for their communities.

# Contents

# Story pictures

Long ago, most people did not learn to read and write. Instead, they listened to stories and learned about ideas and events from what other people told them, or through pictures.

The Ancient Greeks illustrated scenes from myths on vases and plates, and carved the heroes in marble and wood.

In the Middle Ages, people in Europe were taught about the Bible through the stories carved in stone around the entrance to churches, or on the stained-glass windows inside.

In India, several hundred years ago, storytellers travelled from village to village with an illustrated scroll that unfolded to show scenes from great epics. In the East, epic stories were often performed as puppet plays.

In many cases, stories were illustrated on walls, rugs, tapestries, cups and plates and even on clothes. Today, you can read stories in books or watch them on television or at the cinema. All kinds of stories are also told in cartoons.

Ballets and operas also tell exciting stories. Music and mime help to explain the plots which are sometimes quite long and complicated.

Pictures can say as much, if not more, than words. The six main pictures in this book each tell a wonderful story. There is the embroidered story of a real battle that took place almost a thousand years ago; a Russian fairy tale about a frog princess and the brave prince who rescued her; a magical tale of love and confusion by Shakespeare; an ancient Indian saga about a royal prince and a wicked demon.

There is also a fable painted on a plate and the enchanting story of Cinderella.

You may find that the pictures which illustrate these stories don't match up with the ones you have in your head.

Use all the techniques shown in the book to illustrate your versions of these stories and then try creating pictures of your own favourite stories.

# Tales in a tapestry

 The Bayeux Tapestry was made over 900 years ago and is like a huge strip cartoon. The pictures embroidered on it tell the story of one of the most famous battles in history, called the Battle of Hastings, and all the events that led up to it. It was fought between King Harold of England and William, Duke of Normandy.

The Bayeux Tapestry 11th Century. By special permission of the City of Bayeux

The tapestry shows men hunting, farming, feasting, meeting friends and building ships and castles, as well as the fierce fighting between the two armies. To protect themselves, the soldiers carry shields and wear chain-mail armour and helmets with long nose-pieces.

This picture, near the end of the tapestry, shows the death of King Harold. Nobody knows whether Harold is the man with the arrow in his eye or the soldier being struck by a Norman knight. The border at the bottom shows men collecting weapons from dead soldiers.

# The Bayeux Tapestry story

Long ago in England there lived a king called Edward the Confessor, who had no children to take his place when he died. Many people thought they had a right to become the next king. One of them was the King's cousin, William, Duke of Normandy. He claimed that Edward had promised him the throne.

Edward sent his brother-in-law, Harold, to meet William. The two powerful warriors became good friends, but when King Edward became ill he called Harold back to England to help him rule.

When Edward died, Harold was crowned King of England. William was very angry as he felt that Harold had deceived him. He decided to fight Harold for the throne.

William loaded up boats with soldiers and horses and sailed to England to fight Harold at Hastings.

Harold and his men fought bravely, but they were no match for William's strong army. They were defeated and Harold was killed. William became King of England on Christmas Day, 1066. From that day on he was known as William the Conqueror.

# Battleground bravery

The Bayeux Tapestry was sewn by skilled needlewomen, using many different stitches, but only eight colours. It would probably take days, or even weeks, to draw all the people, animals and events it shows. Here are several different ways of making your own Bayeux-style pictures.

## Stitched shield

Make a coloured sketch of a shield like one of those used by the soldiers in the tapestry. Design a bold pattern or fancy initials for it, or draw a picture of a fierce animal to frighten away enemies. Stitch the outline of your shield on a square of felt. Sew the details in different coloured threads and stitches.

## Colossal collage

Make a collage of a fierce battle scene. Use a large piece of pale felt for the background. Cut out soldiers with felt faces and shiny fabric armour. Stick on felt eyes and mouths and any other details. Use fleecy or furry material for horses and stick on woolly manes and tails.

Glue everything on to the background and then add cocktail stick spears and flagpoles.

## Story strip

Make your own comic strip of the Norman invasion. Cut two pieces of paper in half and glue the four strips together. Draw one part of the story in each strip with a decorated border along the top and bottom.

# An Indian epic

The Ramayana is an ancient and famous
Indian saga. Centuries ago, this long
and exciting tale about Rama,
a blue-skinned prince, was told by
storytellers. In the 3rd century BC,
a poet called Valmiki wrote it down.
Later, the story was shown in exquisitely
detailed pictures so that people who
could not read could follow the tale.

Sanskrit illumination for the Ramayana, The British Library, London

There are over 400 pictures in the
series that this painting comes from.
Often a team of artists worked for
years on the illustrations for rich
kings. The master artist sketched
each drawing and lesser artists
filled in the colours.

This picture shows the part of the
story when Rama was living in the
forest. He is having a meal with his
wife, Princess Sita, and his brother,
Lakshmana. Bows and arrows hang
on the hut ready for the two princes
to go out hunting for deer.

## Rama's story

A long time ago, in India, there lived a prince, called Rama. His jealous stepmother had him banished because she wanted her own son to be the next king. For 14 years, Rama lived deep in the forest with his wife, Princess Sita, and his brother, Lakshmana.

One day an evil ten-headed demon, called Ravana, sent a golden deer to lure Prince Rama away from Sita.

Ravana kidnapped the princess and flew off with her in his chariot. On the way to the demon's palace on the island of Lanka, Sita threw out her jewels hoping that Rama would find them and come to rescue her.

Rama and Lakshmana searched all over India until they came to the land of the monkeys. They made friends with Hanuman, the monkey leader, who found Sita's jewels and told Rama where she was being held captive.

With the help of the monkeys, Rama and Lakshmana built a bridge across the dangerous sea and marched to Lanka. After days and nights of fierce battle, Rama killed Ravana and rescued his faithful Princess Sita.

At last it was time for Rama to return home and take his place as king. His loyal subjects lit hundreds of oil lamps to guide their hero back to his kingdom.

# Devilish tricks

Imagine what Ravana, the evil demon, looked like and then create one or all of his ten ugly heads. Or you might like to paint or print a delicately patterned picture of the part of Prince Rama's story that you enjoyed the most.

## Ugly Ravana

Draw the outline of one of Ravana's ugly heads on a piece of stiff card. Mix a sickly shade of green poster paint and add some flour to make it really thick. Paint the head with the mixture and let it dry.

Paint or glue hideous features on to the face. You could use scrunched-up tissue paper for eyes, a lavatory roll for the nose, a sponge for a lolling tongue, silver foil for horns and black wool for hair.

## Indian images

Use felt-tip pens, paints or crayons, to illustrate any part of Prince Rama's story. Fill the paper with bright colours, busy figures and animals. Use lots of delicate patterns for the leaves, clothes and flowers.

## Printed princess

Collect several different things for making prints, such as a cork, sponge, kitchen cloth, potato cuts or cauliflower florets cut in half. Using poster paints, practise printing with each one to see what different shapes and textures they make.

Now create a printed picture – maybe of Princess Sita in a beautiful dress wearing her jewels, or the furry monkeys helping Rama to build the bridge. When the paint is dry, outline the figures in black.

# Pictures on a plate

The pattern on this plate looks Chinese, but it was made in England. It is one of the best-known designs in the world and is called the 'willow pattern'. If you look closely, you can see the pictures that tell a sad story set in China.

*Spode willow pattern plate, about 1790, by courtesy of Spode, Stoke-on-Trent*

The Chinese were the first people to paint patterns on porcelain in this colour, cobalt blue. When this plate was made, Chinese things were very fashionable in Europe. Many factories, including Spode in England, copied Chinese designs and put them on to plates, bowls and dishes, using transfers.

The willow pattern was based on a Chinese design that showed a beautiful landscape. To make it more interesting, Josiah Spode added the three people going over the bridge, as well as the long fence. Several people looked at the willow pattern and made up their own stories to fit the pictures.

# The willow pattern story

A long time ago in China there lived a rich man, called T'so Ling, who had a beautiful daughter, Koong Shee. Although they lived in a magnificent palace with wonderful gardens, Koong Shee was very lonely. Her only friend was the gardener, Chang. The two soon fell in love.

When Koong Shee's father found out about them, he was very angry and sent Chang away for ever. He arranged for Koong Shee to marry a rich old man and he locked her in a small house from which there was no escape. Every day her tears fell into the river like the leaves from the nearby weeping willow tree.

On the night before her wedding, Chang arrived in a boat. He and Koong Shee ran away taking with them a big box of jewels. Koong Shee's father chased them over a bridge but the lovers ran too fast for him and managed to escape.

For many years they lived happily on a nearby island until, one day, Koong Shee's father discovered them. He threw them into a dark maze where they died.

The gods knew how much Koong Shee and Chang had loved each other. They turned their spirits into a pair of doves so they could fly together forever above the weeping willow tree.

# Blue and white pictures

Imagine, like Koong Shee, that you have entered the blue and white world of the willow pattern. Use the ideas of the original story or make up your own, to create a plate painted with pictures and patterns.

## Painted plates

Decide which parts of the willow pattern story you want to show and then draw them in pencil on a white card circle. Draw a patterned border around the edge.

Put blue and white paint on to a palette, or into two separate pots. Mix a little of each in different amounts to make all sorts of shades of blue. The more white you add, the paler the blue will become. Paint your story, using a fine-tipped paintbrush so you can put in lots of details and patterns.

## Willow wax wash

With a dark blue wax crayon, draw your favourite part of the willow pattern story on a sheet of paper. Mix a little pale blue paint with water. Brush it all over the picture. The waxy picture will shine through the paint.

## Black and blue

Cover a white card circle with a thick layer of blue poster paint and leave it to dry. When you are sure it is dry, cover the blue paint with a thick layer of dark blue paint. While the dark blue paint is still wet, use a cotton bud to draw a scene from the willow pattern story.

# Rags to riches

This illustration of Cinderella is by an English artist, called Arthur Rackham. He became famous for his illustrations of fairy tales and children's stories.

Arthur Rackham Illustration for Cinderella by C.S. Evans, 1919

Early in the 1900s, when Rackham painted this illustration, colour printing had only recently been invented. Colour pictures were printed on shiny paper separately from the pages of the story and stuck into the books by hand.

Rackham used four main colours – brown, black, green and red – to show how sad Cinderella is feeling. Since she is the main character, she is painted in great detail. Everyone else is painted as a black shape, known as a silhouette.

# The story of Cinderella

There was once a beautiful girl called Cinderella who lived with her father, her cruel stepmother and two unkind stepsisters. All day long she cooked and cleaned for them, dressed in rags and fed only on scraps, but she never once complained.

One day, an invitation came for everyone in the house to attend the King's ball. Poor Cinderella was not allowed to go. She was made to spend every spare minute sewing her ugly sisters' new ballgowns. On the day of the ball, her excited sisters got ready and went off to the ball in a fine coach.

Cinderella sat crying by the fire, wishing she could go to the ball too. All of a sudden, her fairy godmother appeared. With a swish of her magic wand, she turned a pumpkin into a coach and mice into horses, and gave Cinderella a beautiful silver dress and a pair of fine sparkling slippers. She told Cinderella to be home by midnight, when the spell would wear off.

When Cinderella arrived at the ball no one knew who she was. The Prince fell in love with her immediately, and danced with her all night. However, when the clock struck twelve, Cinderella rushed out of the ballroom, dropping one of her slippers on the palace steps. The Prince took the slipper to every house in the land to find its owner. When he came to Cinderella's house, the ugly sisters rushed to try the slipper on, but it was too small for them. Cinderella's foot, however, was the perfect fit. The happy prince asked her to marry him and she did.

# Midnight magic

Create your own illustrations to go with the story of Cinderella. Once you have tried the different techniques, you might like to use all three together, as Rackham did, to make one incredible picture.

## Handsome prints

Choose a simple shape from the story, such as a glass slipper, a mouse or a royal crown. Practise drawing it until you have a strong, realistic outline.

With a black felt-tip pen, draw this shape on a thin, flat sponge and then carefully cut it out. Glue it on to a square of cardboard. Let the glue dry before you start printing.

Dampen the sponge shape and cover it with poster paint. Press it, paint face down, on to a piece of brightly coloured card. Repeat this until you have a page covered with prints.

## Shadow play

Using white chalk, draw the outlines of Cinderella and other characters from the story on black card.

Carefully cut out the figures and arrange them on a sheet of white paper. Glue them in position, chalky side down. Add details, such as a hat, a pair of gloves or a bow, in different coloured card.

## Hopes and dreams

In his picture, Rackham has made Cinderella look sad because she could not go to the ball. He has chosen sad, dark colours that match her miserable mood.

Think about the colours which best match each part of the story. They could be bright and sparkling for the moment where the prince finds Cinderella, clashing for the two ugly sisters, or pale for Cinderella's moonlit dash to the ball.

Paint a picture in which the figures tell the story and the colours describe the mood.

# Summer dreams

Marc Chagall was a Russian artist, but he spent much of his life travelling and working in France. He often used the memories of his childhood mixed with dreams and Russian folklore to create his exotic pictures, mosaics, stained-glass windows and intricate tapestries.

Marc Chagall, Midsummer Night's Dream, 1939, Musée de Grenoble

This painting was inspired by a play called 'A Midsummer Night's Dream'. It was written about 400 years ago by William Shakespeare, the most famous English playwright.

Chagall liked the play so much that he read it over and over again. The picture shows beautiful Queen Titania, and her lover, Bottom. He was a man with a donkey's head.

## The story of 'A Midsummer Night's Dream'

Deep in an enchanted wood, lived Oberon, King of the fairies, and his beautiful Queen, Titania. One day, King Oberon decided to play a cruel trick on Titania because she had quarrelled with him.

While Titania slept, the King squeezed magic juice on her eyelids. This made her fall in love with the first thing she saw when she woke up – a man, called Bottom, who had been given a donkey's head by Puck.

As Titania lovingly stroked Bottom's furry face, two lovers, called Hermia and Lysander, ran past her into the woods. They were being chased by Demetrius, who wanted to marry Hermia. Close behind him came Helena, who loved Demetrius dearly, though he did not love her!

Seeing them all in such a muddle, King Oberon ordered his helper, Puck, to drop the magic juice into Demetrius's eyes so that he might fall in love with Helena. By mistake, Puck put the drops into Lysander's eyes instead. Quickly, the King charmed Demetrius's eyes as well, and soon both men were hopelessly in love with Helena.

Taking pity on the lovers, King Oberon took the spell off young Lysander who immediately fell back in love with Hermia, leaving Helena to Demetrius. The king also removed the charm from Titania's eyes and she became his loving Queen once more.

# Midsummer muddle

In many of his paintings, Chagall used unrealistic colours and bold shapes; he often showed people and objects floating in the air. Why not let your imagination take over and create your own dream pictures?

### Slumbering Titania

On white sugar paper, draw a picture in pencil of Titania asleep in her bed of flowers, or Hermia and Lysander running away through the woods. Use simple but bold shapes crowded together to give your picture the feeling of a dream.

Wet the paper all over with a paintbrush dipped in water. Dip a fountain pen into Indian ink and trace over your pencil outlines.

When the paper is dry, paint your picture with pale watery colours. It doesn't matter if the colours go over the lines. The more smudgy and blurred your painting is, the more unusual and dreamlike it will look.

## Fairy glade

Collect leaves of different shapes and sizes. Paint the veined side of each leaf a different shade of brown or green. Press the painted leaves on to a big sheet of paper and cover it with multicoloured leaf prints. Let them dry.

Draw some fairies on tracing paper and colour them with wax crayons, using the same colours that you used for the leaves. Cut them out and glue them on to the leafy background.

## Fuzzy feelings

Sketch one of the scenes from 'A Midsummer Night's Dream'. Then draw your picture on the back of coloured gummed paper. Instead of cutting out the shapes, carefully tear along the pencil outlines.

Glue the shapes on to a colourful sheet of paper. The torn edges will give your picture a slightly fuzzy and dreamy look.

# Russian picture box

The tiny picture on this papier mâché box was painted by a Russian artist, called Yagodkina. It shows part of a Russian folk tale which tells the story of Prince Ivan, his frog princess and the evil Kaschey.

Yagodkina, Russian Miniature Box, 1992, Iconastas, London

Long ago in Russia, many artists painted religious pictures, called icons. They worked in large teams and each artist had his own particular job. Some painted only landscapes, others only hands, faces and feet, and some specialised in clothing.

Later, religious worship was forbidden in Russia. Instead of painting icons, artists began to decorate wood, metal and pottery with pictures based on folk tales, songs and history. One artist was allowed to paint a whole picture instead of just a part of it.

# The story of the frog princess

An old Tsar once had three sons. When it was time for them to marry, he told each one to shoot an arrow into the air. Wherever their arrows fell, they would find a wife. Ivan, the youngest prince, was disgusted to find a frog beside his arrow, but he was forced to marry her.

The Tsar held a ball to celebrate the weddings. Prince Ivan waited for his frog princess to arrive, but to his surprise a beautiful girl appeared instead. She explained that her father had cast a spell on her so that she had to spend most of her time as a frog, but soon the spell would wear off. When Prince Ivan got home, he found her discarded frog skin on the floor and quickly burned it. The princess was horrified. Now her father's spell would never be broken. She would have to go to the faraway kingdom of the evil Kaschey.

The prince searched high and low for his princess until he met an old witch who told him that Kaschey lived beneath a huge oak tree. The only way to kill him was to break a needle found in an egg. On his way, Prince Ivan met a bear, a hare, a duck and a big fish. Each, in turn, begged him not to kill them. They promised that, in return, they would help him one day.

Ivan found the tree and wondered how to reach Kaschey. Suddenly, the bear rushed up and knocked the tree over. A stone chest fell from its branches and smashed. The hare ran out of the chest, but it was killed. The duck flew out of the dead hare and dropped an egg into the deep sea. Ivan wept when he realised that the needle must be inside the egg. All at once, the fish rose out of the waves with the egg in its mouth. Ivan grabbed it, snapped the needle inside and Kaschey died instantly. The spell was broken and Ivan and his wife lived happily ever after.

# Merry miniatures

Yagodkina used fine detail and intricate patterns when she painted the picture on her box. You could try and do the same, or you could decorate a bigger box with characters cut out of patterned paper instead.

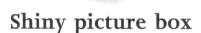

## Shiny picture box

Cover a box with a thick layer of black poster paint. While it is drying, make a simple sketch of one of the characters from the frog princess story, such as Prince Ivan or the duck.

Cut the shapes you need out of patterned paper and shiny sweet wrappers. Arrange them on the top of the black box and then carefully glue the pieces down.

## Painted box

Cover a small box with two thick layers of black poster paint. Use a fine brush to paint a delicate and detailed picture of your favourite character from the story.

When the paint is dry, use a gold felt-tip pen to create a border around your picture and to add details.

## Precious paintings

With bright poster paints and a fine brush, paint a picture from the frog princess story on some black paper. Use as many colours as you like. Let the paint dry.

With a fine gold or silver felt-tip pen, make a patterned frame around your picture. Add details, such as delicate leaves, lattice windows or soft fur.

## Nesting animals

Cut a long strip of white paper and fold it into five equal parts. Paint a chest on the first space making sure that its sides touch the edge of the paper and the first fold. In the next space, draw a hare with its nose touching the chest and its bottom on the second fold.

In the same way, draw a duck, an egg and a needle in the last three spaces. Colour the pictures with felt-tip pens. Carefully cut them out, leaving them attached to each other. Now you have a long strip of pictures which fold one under the other.

# More about the artists and pictures

## The Bayeux Tapestry

(Late 11th Century)

Many people think that Bishop Odo, King William's half-brother, ordered the Bayeux tapestry to be made. He hung it in his cathedral at Bayeux for everyone to see at festivals and on special occasions. It remained there for several centuries, before being seized during the French Revolution and taken to Paris. Now it is back in Bayeux in its own museum. The end of the tapestry seems to have been lost. It would probably have shown William being crowned King of England.

## The Ramayana

(Mid 17th Century)

The illustration of Prince Rama, Princess Sita and Lakshmana comes from the Ayodhyakanda, or second book of the Ramayana. It tells of the life of Rama and Sita in the forest and was completed in Udaipur in 1650. No one knows who painted the 68 pictures in the book but they are likely to be from the studio of Sahib Din. He would probably have sketched the detailed pictures and allowed lesser artists to colour them in.

## The Willow Pattern
(1790)

Although nobody really knows who the artist of the willow pattern was, Thomas Minton may have made the original engraving. He was a fine craftsman who worked for Spode for ten years before setting up his own pottery. At that time, Chinese porcelain was popular in Europe and when, in 1784, tea became cheaper to buy, Spode began to produce Chinese-looking tea sets. Because they were made in England, they were much cheaper than those shipped all the way from China.

## Cinderella
(1919)
Arthur Rackham    1867 - 1939

Arthur Rackham worked as a clerk in a fire office before he became an artist. He quickly became well known for his delicate pictures of children, fairies, and trees that looked almost human. Among the many books he illustrated were Peter Pan, Alice in Wonderland and the fairy stories of Hans Anderson and The Grimm Brothers. At the age of seventy he illustrated his last book – The Wind in the Willows.

## Midsummer Night's Dream
(1939)
Marc Chagall    1887 - 1985

As well as painting pictures, Chagall loved working on large stage sets and designing costumes for the theatre and ballet. The artist, who was Jewish, spent two years working on twelve stained-glass windows for the synagogue at the Hadassah-Hebrew University in Jerusalem. He also designed three huge tapestries to hang on the walls of the Israeli Parliament, and painted enormous panels for the ceiling of the Paris Opera House.

## Russian Miniature Box
(1992)
Yagodkina

Yagodkina lives in the town of Palekh in Russia where icon painters have worked since the 12th century. Today their miniatures, most of which are painted by women, are sold all over the world. The artist took ten days to paint the picture on the box. She used a fine paintbrush with only four hairs so that she could paint the intricate details. When she had finished, she covered the box with seven layers of lacquer.

# Other things to do

1 Cut a card circle and decorate it with stickers. Cut some big white card petals. On each one, paint an exciting or important thing that has happened to you. Start with the day you were born. Stick the petals, in order, clockwise around the centre of the flower, so that they tell the story of your life.

2 Design an information poster without any words, so that it could be understood by people all over the world. You could explain the safe way to cross a road, how to look after pets, or why it is important to brush your teeth every day. Draw several pictures to get your message across clearly.

3 Choose one of your favourite stories or make up a story of your own. Try to tell the story in one picture, rather like the willow pattern story. Include pictures of each of the places and people in the story. You might like to draw your story on a paper plate and decorate the edge with a patterned border.

4 Create your own storybook, by putting eight strips of paper one on top of the other. Fold them in half and sew them together along the fold. Write part of a story on each page. Illustrate them, using a different technique for each one, such as paint, wax resist, silhouette and collage. Design an eye-catching cover.

# Index

## Acknowledgements

*The publishers are grateful to the following institutes and individuals for permission to reproduce the illustrations on the pages mentioned.*
The Harvest, 1989, Peruvian Arpillera, kindly lent by Sandy Adirondack: cover; The Bayeux Tapestry - 11th Century. By special permission of the City of Bayeux: 6; Sanskrit illumination for the Ramayana, The British Library, London (15296F.71r): 10; Spode willow pattern plate, by courtesy of Spode, Stoke-on-Trent: 14; Marc Chagall, Midsummer Night's Dream, 1939, Musée de Grenoble / © ADAGP, Paris and DACS, London, 1996: 22; Yagodkina, Russian Miniature Box, 1992, Iconastas, London: 26.